T0054232

The Great
Panda Tale

FIRST EDITION
Series Editor Deborah Lock; **US Senior Editor** Shannon Beatty; **Editor** Nandini Gupta;
Project Art Editor Hoa Luc; **Production Editor** Francesca Wardell; **Assistant Art Editor** Yamini Panwar;
DTP Designer Anita Yadav; **Picture Researcher** Aditya Katyal;
Deputy Managing Editor Soma Chowdhury; **Design Consultant** Shefali Upadhyay;
Reading Consultant Linda Gambrell, PhD

THIS EDITION
Editorial Management by Oriel Square
Produced for DK by WonderLab Group LLC
Jennifer Emmett, Erica Green, Kate Hale, *Founders*

Editors Grace Hill Smith, Libby Romero, Michaela Weglinski;
Photography Editors Kelley Miller, Annette Kiesow, Nicole DiMella; **Managing Editor** Rachel Houghton;
Designers Project Design Company; **Researcher** Michelle Harris; **Copy Editor** Lori Merritt;
Indexer Connie Binder; **Proofreader** Larry Shea; **Reading Specialist** Dr. Jennifer Albro;
Curriculum Specialist Elaine Larson

Published in the United States by DK Publishing
1745 Broadway, 20th Floor, New York, NY 10019

Copyright © 2023 Dorling Kindersley Limited
DK, a Division of Penguin Random House LLC
23 24 25 26 27 10 9 8 7 6 5 4 3 2 1
001–333439–Apr/2023

All rights reserved.
Without limiting the rights under the copyright reserved
above, no part of this publication may be reproduced, stored
in or introduced into a retrieval system, or transmitted, in any
form, or by any means (electronic, mechanical, photocopying,
recording, or otherwise), without the prior written permission
of the copyright owner.
Published in Great Britain by Dorling Kindersley Limited

A catalog record for this book
is available from the Library of Congress.
HC ISBN: 978-0-7440-6720-0
PB ISBN: 978-0-7440-6721-7

DK books are available at special discounts when purchased
in bulk for sales promotions, premiums, fundraising, or
educational use. For details, contact: DK Publishing Special Markets,
1745 Broadway, 20th Floor, New York, NY 100198
SpecialSales@dk.com

Printed and bound in China

The publisher would like to thank the following for their kind permission to reproduce their images:
a=above; c=center; b=below; l=left; r=right; t=top; b/g=background

Fotolia: Eric Isselee 3, 12; **Shutterstock.com:** Hung Chung Chih 27, gracethang2 18, David Ryo 4-5

Cover images: *Back:* **Fotolia:** Eric Isselee cra, bl; **Getty Images / iStock:** pixhook cla

All other images © Dorling Kindersley

For the curious
www.dk.com

Level

2

The Great Panda Tale

Laura Buller

DK

Contents

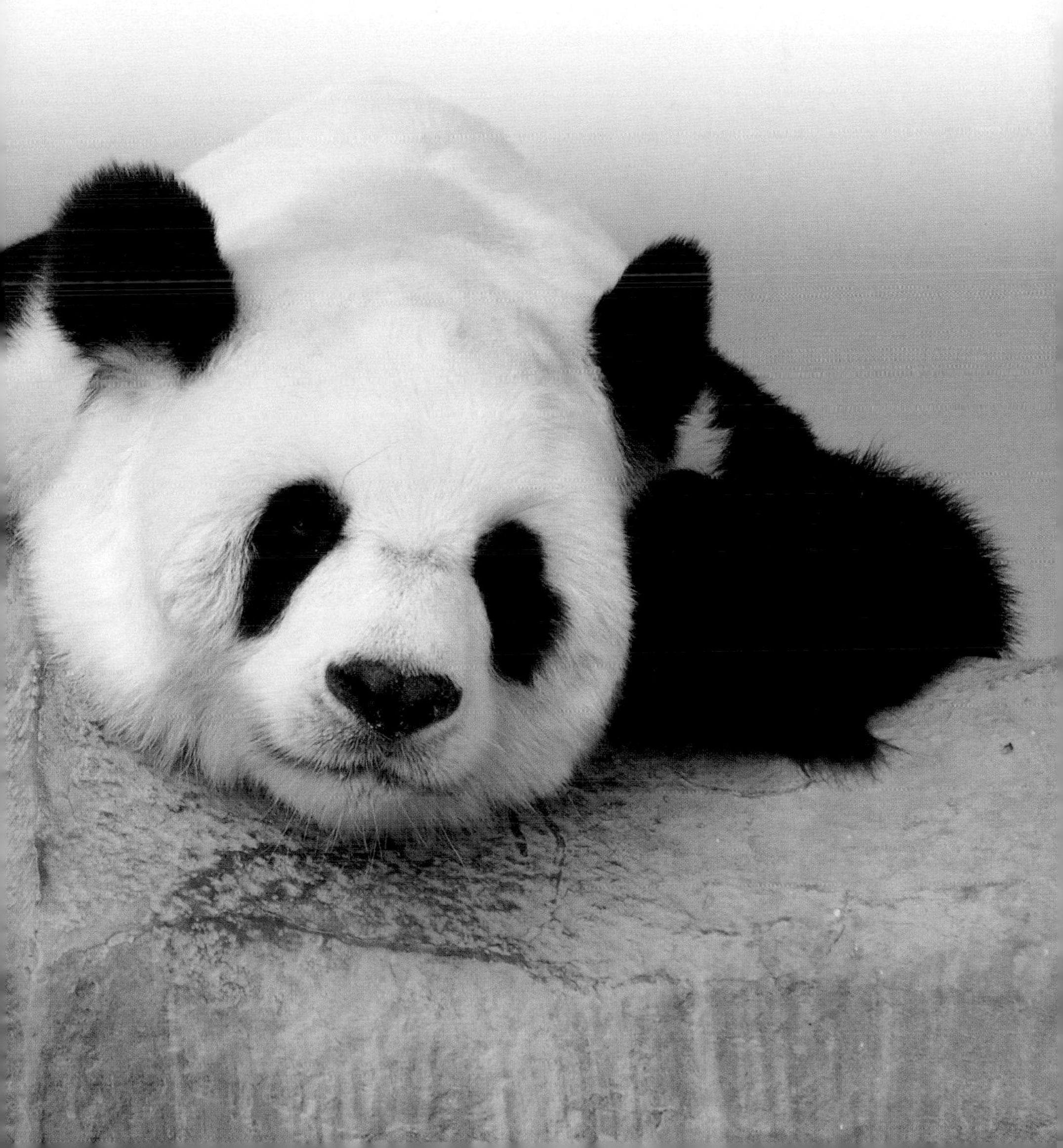

Busy at the Zoo

Do you love learning about and meeting animals?
I am Louise, and since I was a little girl, the zoo has been my favorite place.
It is so exciting to see real animals up close.

Hi, I'm Louise! I'm part of the Zoo Crew.

Roarrr!

I love to watch them move and play and to hear them hoot, growl, and roar.

This year, I did the coolest thing ever. I joined the Zoo Crew. We are kids who help zoo visitors have a great day.

A Panda Mother

This summer, something amazing happened. We found out one of our giant pandas was expecting a baby.

It was big news for the zoo, because no panda cubs had ever been born there.

Panda Habitat

Wild pandas live high up in the mountains of central China. The forests are filled with bamboo plants and trees.

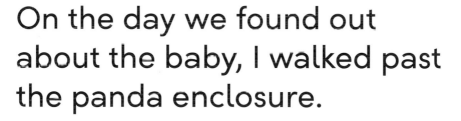

On the day we found out about the baby, I walked past the panda enclosure.

The enclosure is so beautiful. It looks just like the pandas' home in China. I spotted Gao Yun, the male panda, but Zhen Mei, the female, was nowhere to be seen.

When I reached
the research center,
I could barely open the doors.

The place was packed
with people.
Everyone was looking at the
big glass window into the lab.
Zhen Mei was there with
two animal doctors.

I was looking, too, and
bumped right into Ms. Kelly,
the head panda keeper.
I asked her to tell me
what was going on.
She told me the vets were
doing tests on Zhen Mei.
They wanted to find out if
she was going to have a baby.

Happy Birthday!
A panda mother is
pregnant with her baby
for three to five months.
Babies are born in late
summer or early fall.

People were buzzing
with excitement.
A few minutes later,
one vet gave a thumbs-up.
A huge cheer went up.
A new baby panda was on the
way! This was fantastic news
for the whole zoo.

Pandas are vulnerable
animals. There are fewer than
two thousand left in the wild.

Zoos research how to protect wild pandas and help captive pandas have babies.

Caring for Mom

Over the next few months, we took extra care with Zhen Mei. My job was to help provide her main meal: bamboo. A panda chews through a huge pile of bamboo every day.

Pandas need to eat lots of bamboo to keep healthy.

A zookeeper pulls a wagon of bamboo for the panda.

The zookeepers kept
a close eye on how much
Zhen Mei was eating.
They wanted to make sure
her baby was healthy and
growing.

One vet did tests on her poo.
I wouldn't like to have that job!
Zhen Mei needed more time
away from visitors, so they
built her a den.

Around July, we noticed
that Zhen Mei was eating
less bamboo.
She seemed to want to be
alone in the den almost
all the time.
Was it time for the baby
to be born?

First Baby Picture
An ultrasound is a special picture of a baby while still inside its mother.

The vets gave her lots of different tests.
They used an ultrasound machine to see the baby inside her.

Afterward, Ms. Kelly told me that Zhen Mei's cubs looked strong and healthy.
Cubs!
I couldn't believe it.
Our panda mom was going to have twins.

Cubs!

Over the next week, Zhen Mei spent almost all her time in her den.
The zoo team watched her on the panda cam, as she snoozed most of the day.
The vets thought this was a sign the twins were ready to be born.

zzZ

Panda Cam
Zookeepers can keep a constant watch on animals—without disturbing them—by using webcams, like the panda cam.

One morning, the zookeepers heard a strange noise from the panda enclosure. They checked on Zhen Mei. They found her with her new cubs.

The tiny babies were crying for milk.
Soon, the news spread through the zoo.
The babies were here:
a boy and a girl!

Tiny Babies
At birth, a panda weighs
only 3.5 ounces (100 g).
No other mammal has
babies so much smaller
than the adult.

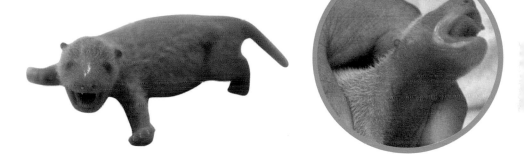

The panda cubs were tiny
enough to cup in your hands.
They were a thousand times
smaller than their mother.
They were pink and wrinkly,
with a few patches of
white hair on their bodies.
Every couple of hours,
they cried to be fed.

The cubs' eyes were
squeezed shut.
They spent most of their time
sleeping and feeding.
This was just like me when
I was a newborn.

Zhen Mei hardly ever put
the babies down.
She cradled them in
her big panda paws.
She sometimes carried one
in her mouth.

The newborn panda is smaller than the zookeeper's hand!

The zookeepers made sure both babies were getting enough to eat.
They had a lot of growing to do!

Each cub drank milk from a bottle.
You could see a row of tiny white teeth when they opened their hungry mouths.

Growing Up

The panda twins were nearly
six weeks old.
I watched them through
a glass window in their nursery.
They were so cute!
Patches of black fur had grown
around their eyes, ears,
shoulders, and little legs.
Their eyes were open now, too.

Little Cloud

Snowdrop

The zoo asked everyone
to choose names for
the new pandas on its website.
People voted for their favorites.
I really liked the winning names:
Little Cloud for the male and
Snowdrop for the female.

At two months old, the cubs
were crawling and would take
their first steps soon.

Panda Names
In Chinese tradition,
babies are named
after 100 days. Pandas
always have Chinese
names. Snowdrop is
Xuehua and Little
Cloud is Xiao Yun.

Little Cloud and Snowdrop began walking when they were around four months old. Little Cloud could even run for a few steps. Snowdrop sometimes climbed on her mother's back for a ride.

Both cubs copied everything their mother did, from climbing trees to eating bamboo. Soon, it would be time for visitors to see the panda twins.

I remember the day Snowdrop
and Little Cloud joined
their mother in the enclosure.

I went to see how they
were doing.
First, I spotted Little Cloud.
He was playing with some
bamboo on the jungle gym.
His sister was looking down
on him from above.

Next, I saw Zhen Mei.
She was keeping an eye
on everyone.
She wanted to keep her
babies safe.
Suddenly, she looked right at
me and waved!

It was the
most amazing end
to an exciting year.

Glossary

Enclosure
An area of land that is surrounded by a wall or fence

Endangered
An animal that is at risk of dying out

Twins
Two babies that are born at the same time during one birth

Ultrasound
A picture of a baby while it is still inside its mother

Veterinarian (vet)
A medical doctor for animals

Index

Quiz

Answer the questions to see what you have learned. Check your answers in the key below.

1. What does the Zoo Crew do?

2. Where do wild pandas live?

3. What do pandas eat?

4. What color were the newborn panda cubs?

5. What do the cubs spend most of their time doing?

1. They help zoo visitors 2. Central China 3. Bamboo
4. Pink 5. Sleeping and feeding